Sociology AS Revision Test Yourself On Family, Education and Research Methods

SOCIOLOGYTWYNHAM.COM

ISBN-13: 978-1507813829
ISBN-10: 1507813821

ACKNOWLEDGEMENT

Special thanks to pixabay.com for allowing the use of their image on the front cover.

CONTENTS

Acknowledgments   i

1   Families and Household Multiple-choice Questions   Pg 1

2   Families and Households Multiple-choice: The Answers   Pg 15

3   Family Single Questions   Pg 21

4   Family Single Questions: The Answers   Pg 23

5   Education Multiple- Choice Questions   Pg 27

6   Education Multiple- Choice Questions: The Answers   Pg 37

7   Education Single Questions   Pg 43

8   Education Single Questions: The Answers   Pg 45

9   Research Methods Multiple-Choice Questions   Pg 49

10   Research Methods Multiple-Choice Questions: The Answers   Pg 58

11   About the author   Pg 63

PLEASE NOTE

This test yourself booklet has been designed so you can assess the extent of your subject knowledge in the multiple-choice questions section and evaluate your understanding in the short questions section.
Our AS-Level revision guide has been designed to accompany this booklet so you can learn from any misunderstandings in order to improve your learning and examination performance.

1 FAMILY - MULTIPLECHOICE QUESTIONS

Q1 - Parsons said the family has two basic functions. These two functions are:

A – the primary socialization of children and the stabilization of children's personalities

B – the stabilization of adult personalities along with the secondary socialization of children

C – the secondary socialization of children and stabilization of children's personalities

D – the primary socialization of children and the stabilization of adult personalities

Q2 – As radical feminists Delphy and Leonard argue it is:

A – women rather than capitalism who benefit the most from exploiting men and the family is central in maintaining this structure

B – men rather than capitalism who benefit the most from exploiting women and the family is central in maintaining this structure

C – men rather than Marxism who benefit the most from exploiting women and the family is central in maintaining this structure

D - men rather than functionalism who benefit the most from exploiting women and the family is central in maintaining this structure

Q3 – In addition, coming from a radical feminist perspective Delphy and Leonard also argue:

A – families are structured; in this structure women dominate while men and children are subordinate (very few families are patriarchal)

B – families are structured; in this structure men dominate while women and children are subordinate (very few families are matriarchal)

C – most families are matriarchal; in this structure women dominate while men and children are subordinate (very few families are patriarchal)

D – families are structured; in this structure men and women are subordinate to children due to the 1989 Children's Act

Q4 - Marxist feminists argue women's oppression benefits capitalism. Benston argues:

A – feminism benefits from a large army of women – an unpaid workforce - who are compliant and willing to do as they're told because women have been socialized to act this way by other women subsequently women rear future workers to think the same way.

B – via the 1989 Children Act, children benefit from a large army of women – an unpaid workforce - who are compliant and willing to do as they're told because women have been socialized to act this way

C – new right thinkers like Charles Murray benefit from a large army of women – an unpaid workforce – who are compliant and willing to do as they're told and form an underclass

D - capitalism benefits from a large army of women – an unpaid workforce - who are compliant and willing to do as they're told because women have been socialized to act this way and women rears future workers to think the same way

Q5 - Marxist and radical feminist both argue the following:

A – Marxist feminists argue the abolition of the family is needed to end women's oppression but radical feminists disagree

B – Both radical and Marxist feminists argue the family is a functional prerequisite and is needed to end women's oppression

C – Both radical and Marxist feminists argue the abolition of the family is needed to end women's oppression

D - Radical feminists argue the abolition of the family is needed to end women's oppression but Marxist feminists disagree

Q6 – New Right perspectives of the family are very similar to those of:

A – Marxist feminists

B – functionalists

C – Marxist

D – Radical feminists

Q7 – "The breadwinner husband and homemaker-wife model is the best structure for self-reliance, reducing the likelihood of welfare dependency" is a statement best attributed to:

A – Benston a Marxist feminist

B - Delphy and Leonard both with radical feminist perspectives

C - John Redwood a Conservative MP with a New Right perspective

D – Zaretsky from a Marxist perspective

Q8 – When discussing pre-industrial families sociologists are referring to a time period:

A – after the industrial revolution

B – during the industrial revolution

C – during the industrial revolution, but on a Friday afternoon

D – before the industrial revolution

Q9 - During the industrialization period the function (purpose) of the family was multifunctional. These functions were:

A - economic production; educational; political and ascribed status

B - economic production; educational and political

C - economic production; educational; political; ascribed status and discipline

D – educational and political

Q10 - Parsons argues the nuclear family best meets the needs of industrial society as it allows individuals to:

A – work hard

B – form a family

C – eat well

D – achieve their status

Q11 – The stabilization of adult personalities occurs via:

A – hard work

B- sexual division of labour

C – economic production

D – ascribed status

Q12 – The instrumental and expressive roles adopted by adults in a nuclear family are known collectively by functionalists as:

A – the dual burden

B – the triple shift

C – matriarchy

D - the sexual division of labour

Q13 – The importance of primary socialization for Parsons is its establishment of:

A – a value consensus

B- the myth of meritocracy

C – the consumption of goods to aid capitalism

D – patriarchal power

Q14 – For Parsons the benefit of the isolated nuclear family is its capacity:

A – in being free from binding obligations to wider kin as well as being geographically and socially mobile

B - in being geographically and socially mobile

C - in being free from binding obligations to wider kin

D – to impose the sexual division of labour without any intrusion from nosey relatives

Q15 – Although Parsons argues the isolated nuclear family was an outcome of industrialization, other sociologists like Laslett disagree because:

A - Laslett argues nuclear families were the norm in pre-industrial England

B – Laslett argues symmetrical families were the norm during industrialization

C - Laslett argues lone parent families were the norm during industrialization

D – Laslett argues same sex families were the norm during pre-industrial England

Q16 - Social policy refers to:

A – government legislation and activities which seek to undermine the wellbeing of its people

B – government legislation and activities which seek to improve the wellbeing of elderly people

C – government legislation and activities which seek to improve the wellbeing of its people

D - to government legislation and activities which seek to improve the wellbeing of just children

Q17 - In 1945 The Welfare State was a social policy set up to allow the state to support families through:

A – welfare benefits and education

B – welfare benefits, housing, the-right-to-vote, health-care and education

C – housing, the-right-to-vote, education and health-care

D – welfare benefits, housing, health-care and education

Q18 - From 1979 the Conservative Government wanted to protect traditional family by introducing a social policy which 'kept tabs on errant fathers'. The agency which was established in 1993 to collect child maintenance payments is known as:

A – Child Welfare Agency (CWA)

B – Children's Income Agency (CIA)

C – Child Support Agency (CSA)

D – Children's Cash Agency (CCA)

Q19 – Feminists' argue all governmental social policies are prejudicial against women because:

A – Conservatives and the New Right social policies seek to keep women in the home while New Labour might recognize family diversity but their social policies see women as being matriarchal

B - Conservatives and the New Right social policies seek to keep women in the home while New Labour might recognize family diversity but their social policies see women as being the primary carer

C – Conservatives and the New Right social policies seek to keep women out of the home while New Labour might recognize family diversity but their social policies see women as being the primary carer

D - Conservatives and the New Right social policies seek to keep men in the home while New Labour might recognize family diversity but their social policies see men as being the primary carer

Q20 - New Right thinkers argue social policies should be designed to support the nuclear family. Feminists are critical of this way of thinking because:

A – the New Right assume the matriarchal nuclear family is 'natural' rather than socially constructed

B – the New Right assume the patriarchal nuclear family is socially constructed

C – the New Right assume matriarchal nuclear family is socially constructed

D – the New Right assume the patriarchal nuclear family is 'natural' rather than socially constructed

Q21 – Giddens argues couples now build their relationships on the quality of their relationships rather than the more traditional obligations of economic dependence or a sense of loyalty. This is known as:

A – confluent love

B – convergent love

C – consistent love

D – conflicted love

Q22 - The characteristics of family diversity identified by *Rapoport and Rapoport* (1982) are:

A – organizational diversity, social-class diversity, family life course diversity and life cycle diversity

B – cultural diversity, social-class diversity, family life course diversity and life cycle diversity

C – cultural diversity, organizational diversity, social-class diversity, family life course diversity and life cycle diversity

D - cultural diversity, health diversity, organizational diversity, social-class diversity, family life course diversity and life cycle diversity

Q23 Gay and lesbian households, single-person households, lone-parent families, dual-worker families and reconstituted families are all examples of:

A – cereal packet families

B- family homogeneity

C – family diversity

D – the dark-side of family life

Q24 – The term cereal packet family is an image giving the impression that most people live in a 'typical family' which:

A – the husband is the 'breadwinner', with a wife who stays at home in order to look after the children and do the housework. Both these parents are married to each other and neither has been married before.

B - the husband is the 'breadwinner', with a wife who stays at home in order to look after the children and do the housework. Both these parents are married to each other but one of them might have been married before.

C - the husband is the 'breadwinner', with a wife who stays at home in order to look after the children and do the housework. Both these parents are married to each other but one of them has been married before bringing their children from the previous relationship with them

D - the husband is the 'breadwinner', with a male 'wife' who stays at home in order to look after the children and do the housework. Both these parents are a same-sex married couple and neither has been married before.

Q25 - Over the past 40 years cohabitation has grown in popularity. Eleanor Macklin identifies 5 motivations for this increase in popularity:

A – affectionate dating, trial marriage, temporary alternative to marriage and permanent alternative to marriage

B – secularization, people wary of marriage, acceptance of cohabitation and women's rights

C – secularization, people wary of marriage, acceptance of cohabitation, gay rights and women's rights

D - temporary casual - for convenience, affectionate dating, trial marriage, temporary alternative to marriage and permanent alternative to marriage

Q26 - Sue Sharpe studied working-class girls in 1970 and found the girls' concerns were marriage, children etc. In 1990 she found girls' priorities had changed to their career and independence. Her findings could help explain the decline decrease in marriage over past 40 years because:

A – it highlighted the growth in secularization

B – it highlighted the acceptance of cohabitation

C – it highlighted the increasing influence of women's rights – focus on career and not being a housewife

D – it highlighted the increasing influence of gay rights

Q27 - The number of births outside marriage has increased to around 50% of all births in 2013. One explanation for this decrease could be due to:

A – The decrease in cohabitation as helped remove the stigma of births inside marriage

B – The growth in cohabitation as helped remove the stigma of births outside marriage

C – The growth in cohabitation as helped increase the stigma of births outside marriage

D - The decrease in cohabitation as helped remove the stigma of births outside marriage

Q28 - Women are having fewer children or having them later in life (in 2013 the average age of becoming a mother increased to 30 years) or indeed remaining childless. One explanation for this increase could be due to:

A – Beck suggests this latter change is due to the decreasing contradiction between women's domestic roles and paid employment

B – Beck suggests this latter change is due to women conducting less domestic roles and more paid employment

C – Beck suggests this latter change is due to women conducting more domestic roles and less paid employment

D - Beck suggests this latter change is due to the increasing contradiction between women's domestic roles and paid employment

Q29 - The number of divorces in the UK have risen sharply since the 1970s with around 42% of all marriages ending in divorce. One explanation for this could be higher expectations of marriage. Allan and Crow explains this as meaning:

A - individuals seek fulfilment from marriage and divorce if it's not found

B - individuals seek nothing particular from marriage and divorce as something to do

C - individuals seek fulfilment from marriage and divorce when fulfilled

D – individuals seek fulfilment from marriage and so divorce so they can remarry

Q30 - The number of divorces in the UK have risen sharply since the 1970s with around 42% of all marriages ending in divorce. One explanation is secularization; secularization is:

A - declining influence of religion on society

B – increasing influence of religion on society

C – static influence of religion on society

D – confirmation of religion never having had any influence on society

Q31 – An empty shell marriage is:

A – where a couple divorces but decide to cohabit

B- where a couple remains legally married but only sexual relations remain

C - where a couple remains legally married but love, sex and companionship are in the past

D - where a couple divorce but love, sex and companionship remain

Q32 - Marxist feminists' argue rising divorce rates are an outcome of the tensions caused by the dual-burden of capitalism. The dual-burden is:

A – where women are forced to undertake unpaid labour at home, while in the workplace they tend to occupy jobs with no wages

B – where women are forced to undertake unpaid labour at home, while in the workplace they tend to occupy jobs with low wages

C – where women are forced to undertake well-paid labour at home, while in the workplace they tend to occupy jobs with low wages

D - where women are forced to undertake unpaid labour at home, while in the workplace they tend to occupy jobs with high wages

Q33 - Radical feminists would point out increasing divorce rates are an outcome of the dark-side of family life being more openly discussed allowing women to:

A – remain in oppressive relationships while protecting children from witnessing violent relationships

B – remain in oppressive relationships but are free to choose whether to work or not

C – leave oppressive relationships as well as protecting children from witnessing violent relationships

D – leave oppressive relationships but return to them when the situation has calmed down

Q34 - The term 'dark side' of the family refers to:

A – a family home having its electricity supply cut-off due to welfare cuts

B – every family member being unemployed and on welfare

C - abuse within the family, particularly towards women and children

D – the continuing increase in divorce rates

Q35 - Elizabeth Bott's 'Family and Social Network' looks at two contrasting types of conjugal roles: segregated and joint. Segregated and joint conjugal roles are:

A – Segregated conjugal roles where husband and wife share tasks. Joint conjugal roles with little or no differentiation between the tasks

B – Segregated conjugal roles involves no clear differentiation between a husband and wife's tasks. Joint conjugal roles with huge differentiation between the tasks

C – Segregated conjugal roles involve a clear differentiation between the tasks undertaken by men and women. Joint conjugal roles where husband and wife share tasks with little or no differentiation between the tasks

D – Segregated and joint conjugal roles is another term used to describe Elizabeth Bott's concept of the sexual division of labour

Q36 - Wilmott and Young's 'The Symmetrical Family' detects a shift in conjugal roles moving away from traditional segregated roles towards more:

A – asymmetrical forms of relationships

B – same sex relationships

C – segregated forms of relationships

D - symmetrical forms of relationships

Q37 - Duncombe and Marsden's research reinforces previous studies revealing inequalities in power and domestic responsibilities. They coined the term the 'triple-shift' to describe the burden placed on women. The term 'triple-shift' refers to:

A – voluntary work, paid work outside the home, housework and emotional work

B – voluntary work, housework and emotional work

C – housework, trouble-free sex and paid work outside the home

D – paid work outside the home, housework and emotional work

Q38 - Married women become economically dependent on their husbands especially as once children arrive women give up work in order to look after the children. Phal's research found the consequence of this on a woman's economic position within a marriage is:

A – the married couple's roles became more symmetrical

B – men tended to control and manage a couple's money

C – women tended to control and manage a couple's money as they were at home all day

D – children tended to be included more in any financial decision making

Q39 - Neil Postman argues childhood is disappearing as children are able to experience things that previously were only available to adults. What term does Postman use to describe the influence of the mass media on the erosion of childhood?

A – Dracula Syndrome

B – Horror Syndrome

C - Frankenstein Syndrome

D – Childhood Syndrome

Q40 – What do you understand by the term child-centeredness:

A – where children put parents first

B – where siblings put each other first

C – where parents put their children first

D – where children put themselves first

2 FAMILY - MULTIPLE CHOICE QUESTIONS: THE ANSWERS

Q1 - Parsons said the family has two basic functions. These two functions are:

D – the primary socialization of children and the stabilization of adult personalities

Q2 – As radical feminists Delphy and Leonard argue it is:

B – men rather than capitalism who benefit the most from exploiting women and the family is central in maintaining this structure

Q3 – In addition, coming from a radical feminist perspective Delphy and Leonard also argue:

B – families are structured; in this structure men dominate while women and children are subordinate (very few families are matriarchal)

Q4 - Marxist feminists argue women's oppression benefits capitalism. Benston argues:

D - capitalism benefits from a large army of women – an unpaid workforce - who are compliant and willing to do as they're told because women have been socialized to act this way and women rears future workers to think the same way

Q5 - Marxist and radical feminist both argue the following:

C – Both radical and Marxist feminists argue the abolition of the family is needed to end women's oppression

Q6 – New Right perspectives of the family are very similar to those of:

B – functionalists

Q7 – "The breadwinner husband and homemaker-wife model is the best structure for self-reliance, reducing the likelihood of welfare dependency" is a statement best attributed to:

C - John Redwood a Conservative MP with a New Right perspective

Q8 – When discussing pre-industrial families sociologists are referring to a time period:

D – before the industrial revolution

Q9 - During the industrialization period the function (purpose) of the family was multifunctional. These functions were:

A - economic production; educational; political and ascribed status

Q10 - Parsons argues the nuclear family best meets the needs of industrial society as it allows individuals to:

D – achieve their status

Q11 – The stabilization of adult personalities occurs via:

B- sexual division of labour

Q12 – The instrumental and expressive roles adopted by adults in a nuclear family are known collectively by functionalists as:

D - the sexual division of labour

Q13 – The importance of primary socialization for Parsons is its establishment of:

A – a value consensus

Q14 – For Parsons the benefit of the isolated nuclear family is its capacity:

A – in being free from binding obligations to wider kin as well as being geographically and socially mobile

Q15 – Although Parsons argues the isolated nuclear family was an outcome of industrialization, other sociologists like Laslett disagree because:

A - Laslett argues nuclear families were the norm in pre-industrial England

Q16 - Social policy refers to:

C – government legislation and activities which seek to improve the wellbeing of its people

Q17 - In 1945 The Welfare State was a social policy set up to allow the state to support families through:

D – welfare benefits, housing, health-care and education

Q18 - From 1979 the Conservative Government wanted to protect traditional family by introducing a social policy which 'kept tabs on errant fathers'. The agency which was established in 1993 to collect child maintenance payments is known as:

C – Child Support Agency (CSA)

Q19 - Feminists argue all governmental social policies are prejudicial against women because:

B - Conservatives and the New Right social policies seek to keep women in the home while New Labour might recognize family diversity but their social policies see women as being the primary carer

Q20 - New Right thinkers argue social policies should be designed to support the nuclear family. Feminists are critical of this way of thinking because:

D – the New Right assume the patriarchal nuclear family is 'natural' rather than socially constructed

Q21 – Giddens argues couples now build their relationships on the quality of their relationships rather than the more traditional obligations of economic dependence or a sense of loyalty. This is known as:

A – confluent love

Q22 - The characteristics of family diversity identified by *Rapoport and Rapoport* (1982) are:

C – cultural diversity, organizational diversity, social-class diversity, family life course diversity and life cycle diversity

Q23 Gay and lesbian households, single-person households, lone-parent families, dual-worker families and reconstituted families are all examples of:

C – family diversity

Q24 – The term cereal packet family is an image giving the impression that most people live in a 'typical family' which:

A – the husband is the 'breadwinner', with a wife who stays at home in order to look after the children and do the housework. Both these parents are married to each other and neither has been married before.

Q25 - Over the past 40 years cohabitation has grown in popularity. Eleanor Macklin identifies 5 motivations for its increase in popularity:

D - temporary casual - for convenience, affectionate dating, trial marriage, temporary alternative to marriage and permanent alternative to marriage

Q26 - Sue Sharpe studied working-class girls in 1970 and found their concerns were marriage, children etc. In 1990 she found girls' priorities had changed to their career and independence. Her findings could help explain the decline decrease in marriage over past 40 years because:

C – it highlighted the increasing influence of women's rights – focus on career and not being a housewife

Q27 - The number of births outside marriage has increased to around 50% of all births in 2013. One explanation for this decrease could be due to:

B – The growth in cohabitation as helped remove the stigma of births outside marriage

Q28 - women are having fewer children or having them later in life (in 2013 the average age of becoming a mother increased to 30 years) or indeed remaining childless. One explanation for this increase could be due to:

D - Beck suggests this latter change is due to the increasing contradiction between women's domestic roles and paid employment

Q29 - The number of divorces in the UK have risen sharply since the 1970s with around 42% of all marriages ending in divorce. One explanation for this could be higher expectations of marriage. Allan and Crow explains this as meaning:

A - individuals seek fulfilment from marriage and divorce if it's not found

Q30 - The number of divorces in the UK have risen sharply since the 1970s with around 42% of all marriages ending in divorce. One explanation is secularization; secularization is:

A - declining influence of religion on society

Q31 – An empty shell marriage is:

C - where a couple remains legally married but love, sex and companionship are in the past

Q32 - Marxist feminists' argue rising divorce rates are an outcome of the tensions caused by the dual-burden of capitalism. The dual-burden is:

B – where women are forced to undertake unpaid labour at home, while in the workplace they tend to occupy jobs with low wages

Q33 - Radical feminists would point out increasing divorce rates are an outcome of the dark-side of family life being more openly discussed allowing women to:

C – leave oppressive relationships as well as protecting children from witnessing violent relationships

Q34 - The term 'dark side' of the family refers to:

C - abuse within the family, particularly towards women and children

Q35 - Elizabeth Bott's 'Family and Social Network' looks at two contrasting types of conjugal roles: segregated and joint. Segregated and joint conjugal roles are:

C – Segregated conjugal roles involve a clear differentiation between the tasks undertaken by men and women. Joint conjugal roles where husband and wife share tasks with little or no differentiation between the tasks

Q36 - Wilmott and Young's 'The Symmetrical Family' detects a shift in conjugal roles moving away from traditional segregated roles towards more:

D - symmetrical forms of relationships

Q37 - Duncombe and Marsden's research reinforces previous studies revealing inequalities in power and domestic responsibilities. They coined the term the 'triple-shift' to describe the burden placed on women. The term 'triple-shift' refers to:

D – paid work outside the home, housework and emotional work

Q38 - Married women become economically dependent on their husbands especially as once children arrive women give up work in order to look after the children. Phal's research found the consequence of this on a woman's economic position within a marriage is:

B – men tended to control and manage a couple's money

Q39 - Neil Postman argues childhood is disappearing as children are able to experience things that previously were only available to adults. What term does Postman use to describe the influence of the mass media on the erosion of childhood?

C - Frankenstein Syndrome

Q40 – What do you understand by the term child-centeredness:

C – where parents put their children first

3 FAMILY - SINGLE QUESTIONS

Q1 Identify one reason why women today might delay having children

Q2 Identify one reason why the lives of children are seen to have improved over the past 100 years

Q3 Identify one reason why ethnic diversity over the past 50 years has increased family diversity

Q4 Identify one reason which illustrates how the difference between children and adults has narrowed

Q5 Identify one reason why the number of first-time marriages are in decline

Q6 Identify one reason why women might have less children than 50 years ago

Q7 Identify one reason for increasing life expectancy

Q8 Identify two effects of women undertaking paid work on a couple's relationship

Q9 Identify two changing functions of the family

Q10 Identify two features of the symmetrical family

Q11 Identify two ways in which industrialization changed the lives of children

Q12 Identify two influences which could explain the growth in family diversity

Q13 Identify two criticisms of functionalist views of the family

Q14 Identify two criticisms of Marxist views of the family

Q15 Identify two criticisms of feminist views of the family

Q16 Identify two criticisms of radical feminist views of the family

Q17 Identify four ways in which feminist sociologists have aided our understanding of family dynamics

Q18 Identify four reasons for the for the changes in family size over the past 100 years

4 **FAMILY** – SINGLE QUESTIONS: THE ANSWERS

Q1 Identify one reason why women today might delay having children

- age at which women start having a family is rising
- women are delaying starting a family to pursue a career
- rising costs mean couples prefer to save first
- the availability of IVF and other reproductive technology 'extends' the delay
- more women are going to university and other educational opportunities

Q2 Identify one reason why the lives of children are seen to have improved over the past 100 years

- improved overall health
- improved diet and nutrition
- improved health care and associated treatments
- families more child-centred
- more rights for children
- improved education opportunities

Q3 Identify one reason why ethnic diversity over the past 50 years has increased family diversity

- more extended families
- diverse attitudes to marriage
- differing parent/child relationships
- number of children in a family
- differing attitudes to divorce
- differing relationships between husband and wife

Q4 Identify one reason which illustrates how the difference between children and adults has narrowed

- children have greater access to the adult world especially via Internet
- the difference between adult and youth culture has narrowed with parents accompanying their teenage children to concerts
- aspects of social media like Facebook and Instagram are enjoyed by children and their parents for example teenagers have their parents as 'friends'
- children are increasingly economically dependent on their parents much later in life; for example children living at parental home much longer meaning the parent can still 'see' their 25 year-old offspring as a child
- lifelong learning is extending childhood for example children can now continue studying late into their twenties so the parent is still 'looking-after' their offspring

Q5 Identify one reason why the number of first-time marriages are in decline

- cohabitation has become an accepted alternative to marriage
- men are increasingly becoming fearful of divorce settlements going in a woman's favour
- some remarriages can involve people who have never married before
- less stigma associated with singlehood
- increase in divorce rates can make a couple wary of marriage

Q6 Identify one reason why women might have less children than 50 years ago

- less stigma associated with being childless
- greater career opportunities
- greater costs in bringing up children
- increased child-centredness puts a greater burden on the woman
- more availability of contraception and morning-after pill
- women defer having children to much later in life

Q7 Identify one reason for increasing life expectancy

- improved health-care facilities
- improved/better awareness of healthier diet
- improved/better awareness of health education
- improved sanitation
- improved/better awareness of available hospital treatments/medicines
- improved/better awareness of working-conditions

Q8 Identify two effects of women undertaking paid work on a couple's relationship

- gender scripts – socially constructed expectations of roles within the family could be challenged with man/husband having to do more child-care
- changing financial controls – man/husband giving up complete control
- emotional labour – child-care could become shared between husband and wife
- decision making – this could become shared between husband/wife
- divorce – added strain of wife being out at work further career could empower her to file for divorce or husband could become disgruntled and file for divorce
- expressive and instrumental roles – these could reverse with dad staying at home while wife becomes breadwinner
- dark-side of the family – wife's new role and confidence could make male partner/husband jealous and he becomes violent (domestic violence)

Q9 Identify two changing functions of the family

- social control of its members
- education
- primary and secondary socialization
- reproduction of children
- nurturing of children
- passing on property
- family was once responsible for health-care and welfare provision

Q10 Identify two features of the symmetrical family

- women in paid employment
- men helping with domestic/housework work such as washing-up
- couples sharing childcare
- couples sharing decision making
- couples sharing leisure time

Q11 Identify two ways in which industrialization changed the lives of children

- compulsory schooling/education means adult's responsibility for looking after their children is increasing
- children given rights in law as well as increasing child-centredness
- fall in infant mortality rates as well as birthrates means it's easier for a parent to focus their attention on one child than several (child-centredness)
- the mass media have turned their attention on children with dedicated programmes in addition mass media has narrowed the gap between adult and children's entertainment e.g. social media
- children are targeted by big business making them consumers in their own right e.g. pester-power

Q12 Identify two influences which could explain the growth in family diversity

- confluent love
- ageing population
- increasing divorce rates
- changing women's position
- gay rights movement
- secularization of society
- increasing trends in cohabitation
- increasing trends in singlehood
- social and legal recognition of same sex relations

Q13 Identify two criticisms of functionalist views of the family

- Murdock's views of the family are value laden, they are prejudicial against women and anti-family diversity
- ignores the dark-side of the family
- Willmott and Young – the extended family still exists which goes against the idea industrialization gave rise to the emergence of the nuclear family and it being geographically mobile

Q14 Identify two criticisms of Marxist views of the family

- the Marxist view that capitalism is unjust is rejected by many sociologists
- sociologists agree the family is influenced by economic system, however most disagree the family is shaped by its needs

Q15 Identify two criticisms of feminist views of the family

- feminists ignore the positive aspects of family life as many women enjoy running a home and bringing up children
- feminists ignore the rise of gender equality in areas of equal pay allowing women more say in decision making within the family
- there is evidence of greater gender equality within the home, with a small but increasing number of men becoming househusbands

Q16 Identify two criticisms of radical feminist views of the family

- some families are matriarchal as opposed to being patriarchal
- ignores the role of capitalism in oppressing women
- some men support the women's movement and its associated rights
- it ignores the advances made in women's rights on issues such as equal pay
- it ignores the class differences in women's position, the higher the social-class of women the greater their rights

Q17 Identify four ways in which feminist sociologists have aided our understanding of family dynamics

- the triple-shift
- the dual burden
- trouble free sex
- the emasculation of women through emotional responsibilities
- women's economic dependency on men
- patriarchal power on decision making

Q18 Identify four reasons for the for the changes in family size over the past 100 years

- geographic mobility
- influence of feminism
- dual-worker households
- child-centredness
- cost of raising children
- changes in infant mortality
- changes in social policy on welfare payments
- contraception
- changing role of women

5 **EDUCATION** - MULTIPLE CHOICE QUESTIONS

Q1 The 1944 Education Act established 3 types of schools. This system was known as:

A – the triple system

B- marketization system

C – the tripartite system

D – the post-war system

Q2 The 1944 Education Act established particular types of schools:

A – public schools; fee-paying schools and independent schools

B – Free Schools; Academy Schools and Specialist Schools

C – state schools; comprehensive and Grammar Schools

D – secondary modern schools; secondary technical schools; Grammar Schools

Q3 Comprehensive schools are school which have:

A – no selection test

B – a selection test

C – the 11+ test

D – selection based on parental income

Q4 Comprehensive schools were introduced in order to:

A - reduce social class divisions and break-down social-class barriers

B – increase class divisions and construct social-class barriers

C – reduce social class barriers and introduce marketization of education

D – increase social class barriers and eliminate the marketization of education

Q5 - The 1988 Education Reform Act introduced:

A - competition between schools and turned parents into 'consumers' of education

B – competition between fee-paying schools and turned parents into 'consumers' of education

C – the post-code lottery so schools would compete with each other

D – removed the post-code lottery so schools would no longer compete with each other

Q6 – The 1988 Education Act introduced several educational polices. Three of these are:

A - Comprehensive schools: Ofsted and open enrolment and parental choice

B - Grammar Schools; secondary modern schools and the tripartite system

C - National Curriculum; Ofsted: open enrolment and parental choice

D - secondary modern schools; secondary technical schools; Grammar Schools

Q7 – Writing over 100 years' ago Durkheim argued the main function of education was to bind members of society together. Therefore the education system is:

A – a social adhesive

B - a dysfunctional perquisite

C - a function of society

D – a functional perquisite

Q8 For functionalists one of the key functions of the education system is:

A – to cultivate ascribed status

B – to cultivate achieved status

C – to nurture primary socialization

D – to prevent meritocracy

Q9 - Althusser (Marxist) argued that the main role of education in a capitalist society was the reproduction of:

A - an anti-meritocratic ideology

B – anti-school subcultures

C – an efficient and obedient work force

D – an inefficient and disobedient work force

Q10 – Bowles and Gintis (Marxists) came up with the concept of 'the correspondence principle'. The correspondence principle recognizes:

A - a school's processes are very dissimilar to offices and factories

B - schools legitimate the myth that everyone has an equal chance

C - school processes recognize the myth of meritocracy

D - a school's processes are very similar to those found in offices and factories

Q11 Both functionalist and Marxist perspectives have similarities. They both:

A - tend to ignore social processes within school – except Willis

B - tend to ignore social processes outside school – except Willis

C - tend to ignore social processes in and outside school – except Willis

D - tend to ignore social processes within school – except Willis

Q12 – Which term does Bourdieu use to describe the cultural characteristics and values of each social class?

A – deviancy amplification

B – habitus

C- myth of meritocracy

D - counter-culture

Q13 – Cultural capital as identified by Bourdieu refers to:

A – pupil premium

B – deferred gratification

C – the knowledge, language and values which readily translate into educational capital

D – present time orientation

Q14 – Cultural differences are extended further by examining sub-cultural differences between social groups. Sugarman and Hyman highlighted the effects of socialization because:

A – the middle classes socialized their children to have present time orientation and deferred gratification

B - the middle classes socialized their children to have future time orientation and immediate gratification

C - the middle classes socialized their children to have present time orientation and immediate gratification

D - the middle classes socialized their children to have future time orientation and deferred gratification

Q15 – Bernstein's research focused on linguistic deprivation and is influence on educational success. Bernstein distinguished between:

A – academic speeches codes and non-academic speech codes

B – educational speech codes and vocational speech codes

C – restricted speech codes and elaborated speech codes

D – compensatory speech codes and pupil premium speech codes

Q16 – Pupil premium is used by the state as a form of:

A – compensatory education

B – fatalism

C – homework policy

D – streaming

Q17 - Rutter places great emphasis on the way a school organizes itself. The better their organizational structures and polices the better the school. Three of these policies are:

A – streaming; setting and assemblies

B- setting; homework policy; and sports day

C - marking policy; teacher reward systems; mixed ability classes

D – mixed ability classes; Maths lessons; English lessons

Q18 – Bowles and Ginitis talk of the myth of meritocracy. The myth of meritocracy refers to:

A – schools make sure all students are aware only a select number of people will ever succeed

B – schools tell students failure is a myth

C - schools legitimate the myth that everyone has an equal chance

D – schools tell children if you work hard your dreams will come true

Q19 – The difference between setting and streaming is:

A - setting is where pupils of similar ability are put in different sets (groups) in specific subjects studied, while streaming involves grouping students of similar ability for every subject studied

B – setting is where pupils of different ability are put in different groups/sets in some subjects studied, while streaming involves grouping students of similar ability for every subject studied

C - setting is where pupils of similar ability are put in different groups/sets in specific subjects studied, while streaming involves grouping students of different ability for every subject studied

D - setting is where pupils of different ability are put in different groups/sets in some subjects studied, while streaming involves grouping students of similar ability for some subject studied

Q20 – The halo effect is positive stereotype given by teachers to pupils who:

A – are seen as lazy and troublesome

B – have a 'culture of resistance' to school life

C – are enthusiastic and hardworking

D - form anti-school subcultures

Q21 - Rosenthal and Jacobson's (1968) research found positive and negative labels helped produce:

A – mixed ability classes

B – self-fulfilling prophecy in the classroom

C – material deprivation

D – setting and streaming

Q22 - Mac an Ghaill (1994) identified 3 working-class male subcultures. These are:

A – macho lads; macho lasses; macho people

B – bright lads; average lads; slow lads

C – academic achievers; average achievers; low achievers

D - macho lads; academic achievers; new enterprisers

Q23 – As well as Paul Willis, Colin Lacey's (1970) study of Hightown Grammar school also showed how streaming can lead to the creation of:

A – halo effect

B – anti-school subculture

C – meritocracy

D – cultural capital

Q24 - C. Jackson (2006) 'Lads and Ladettes in School: Gender and the Fear of Failure' looked at how girls are forming anti-school subcultures and becoming:

A – ladettes because of the fear of boys

B – ladettes because of the fear of academic success

C – ladettes because of the fear of academic failure

D - ladettes because of the fear of PE

Q25 – Complete the sentence: 'Gender is not the strongest predictor of attainment.....'

A – because social class attainment gap at Key Stage 4 is three times as wide as the gender gap and some minority ethnic groups achievement is much greater than the gap between boys and girls.

B – because social class attainment gap at Key Stage 4 is insignificant but some minority ethnic groups achievement is much greater than the gap between boys and girls.

C - because social class attainment gap at Key Stage 4 is three times as wide as the gender gap and some minority ethnic groups achievement is insignificant compared to the gap between boys and girls.

D - because social class attainment gap and some minority ethnic groups achievement is the same as than the gap between boys and girls.

Q26 - Teacher-pupil interaction affecting the gender gap. Howe (1997) identified the different ways teachers interact with boys and girls - such differences in interaction emerge....

A – late, around Key Stage 4

B – very late, around Key Stage 5

C - very early, even in preschool

D – early, even in Key Stage 2

Q27 - Masculine identity can be seen as incompatible with academic success. Kelly (1987) found science and the science classroom remain:

A – gender neutral environments with either gender of teacher dominating science classrooms

B – gender neutral environments with nobody dominating science classrooms

C – 'feminine' environments with girls dominating science classrooms

D - 'masculine' environments with boys dominating science classrooms

Q28 – The term ethnocentric curriculum refers to:

A – the school curriculum and the hidden curriculum is too focused on white British culture and adds to the low self-esteem and underachievement of ethnic minorities

B – the school curriculum and the hidden curriculum is not focused enough on white British culture and adds to the low self-esteem and underachievement of ethnic minorities

C – the hidden curriculum is too focused on white British culture and adds to the low self-esteem and underachievement of ethnic minorities

D - school curriculum is too focused on white British culture and adds to the low self-esteem and underachievement of ethnic minorities

Q29 – Family life outside school can affect achievement inside school. Some minority ethnic groups have stronger parental support than others. Chinese students are seen to have high levels of achievement in school because:

A – Archer (2006) found Chinese students and parents put a high value on education as it gave the family a high standing in their community

B- Archer (2006) found Chinese students and parents put a low value on education as it gave the family a high standing in their community

C - Archer (2006) found Chinese students and parents were indifferent to education as it gave the family a high standing in their community

D - Archer (2006) found Chinese students and parents put a high value on education as it gave the family a no standing in their community

Q30 - Ethnicity and achievement. Identify which of the three statements is correct:

A - Stephen J. Ball (2008) found that Black Caribbean and African students are more likely to be identified for gifted and talented programmes. In contrast, evidence also suggests that Chinese and Indian students are less likely to be entered into higher sets

B - Stephen J. Ball (2008) found that Black Caribbean and African students are less likely to be identified for gifted and talented programmes. Evidence also suggests that Chinese and Indian students are also likely to be entered into lower sets

Continues overleaf

C - Stephen J. Ball (2008) found that Black Caribbean and African students are more likely to be identified for gifted and talented programmes. In addition, evidence also suggests that Chinese and Indian students are more likely to be entered into higher sets

D - Stephen J. Ball (2008) found that Black Caribbean and African students are less likely to be identified for gifted and talented programmes. In contrast, evidence also suggests that Chinese and Indian students are more likely to be entered into higher sets

Q31 – Ethnicity and achievement. Identify which of the three statements is correct:

A - African-Caribbean and Bangladeshi Asians are less likely to be working-class and not in poverty and so have a general material advantage while Indian and African Asian children are more likely to come from professional/business middle-class backgrounds and the subsequent advantages

B - African-Caribbean and Bangladeshi Asians are more likely to be working-class and in poverty and so have a general material disadvantage while Indian and African Asian children are more likely to come from professional/business middle-class backgrounds and the subsequent advantages

C - African-Caribbean and Bangladeshi Asians are more likely to be working-class as are Indian and African Asian children and have a general material disadvantage

D - African-Caribbean and Bangladeshi Asians and Indian and African Asian children are more likely to come from professional/business middle-class backgrounds and the subsequent material advantages

Q32 Ethnicity and attainment. Identify which of the three statements is correct:

A - some ethnic groups, such as Chinese students, have far higher levels of attainment compared to the national level

B – some ethnic groups, such as Chinese students, have far lower levels of attainment compared to the national level

C – some ethnic groups, such as Chinese students, have average levels of attainment compared to the national level

Q33 – Ethnicity and attainment. Identify which of the three statements is correct:

A - Chinese students are the highest attaining group, with 95.5% achieving 5 A*-C grades including Maths and English. This compares to 70% in 2006/07

B - Chinese students are the lowest attaining group, with 38.5% achieving 5 A*-C grades including Maths and English. This compares to 70% in 2006/07

C - Chinese students are the highest attaining group, with 78.5% achieving 5 A*-C grades including Maths and English. This compares to 70% in 2006/07

Q34 - Ethnicity and attainment. Identify which of the four statements is correct:

A - Bangladeshi pupils now have a slightly lower attainment rate than White pupils, with 59.7% 5 A*-C grades including Maths and English. This is a massive improvement given that only around 40% achieved this 2006/07, which was 5% less than White pupils

B - Bangladeshi pupils now have a slightly higher attainment rate than White pupils, with 99.7% 5 A*-C grades including Maths and English. This is a massive improvement given that only around 40% achieved this 2006/07, which was 5% less than White pupils

C - Bangladeshi pupils now have a slightly higher attainment rate than White pupils, with 59.7% 5 A*-C grades including Maths and English. This is a massive improvement given that only around 40% achieved this 2006/07, which was 5% less than White pupils

Q35 – Ethnicity and attainment. Identify which of the four statements is correct:

A - Travellers, Gypsies and Roma are still the highest achieving groups, with 97.5% of Irish Travellers and 90.8% of those from Gypsy or Roma backgrounds achieving 5 A*-C grades including Maths and English.

B - Travellers, Gypsies and Roma are still the lowest achieving groups, with 17.5% of Irish Travellers and 10.8% of those from Gypsy or Roma backgrounds achieving 5 A*-C grades including Maths and English.

C - Travellers, Gypsies and Roma are still the average achieving groups, with 47.5% of Irish Travellers and 50.8% of those from Gypsy or Roma backgrounds achieving 5 A*-C grades including Maths and English.

6 EDUCATION - MULTIPLE CHOICE ANSWERS

Q1 The 1944 Education Act established 3 types of schools. This system was known as:

C – the tripartite system

Q2 The 1944 Education Act established particular types of schools:

D – secondary modern schools; secondary technical schools; grammar schools

Q3 Comprehensive schools are schools which have:

A – no selection test

Q4 Comprehensive schools were introduced in order to

A - reduce social class divisions and break-down social-class barriers

Q5 - The 1988 Education Reform Act introduced

A - competition between schools turning parents into 'consumers' of education

Q6 – The 1988 Education Act introduced several educational polices. Three of these are:

C - National Curriculum; Ofsted: open enrolment and parental choice

Q7 – Writing over 100 years' ago Durkheim argued the main function of education was to bind members of society together. Therefore the education system is

D – a functional perquisite

Q8 For functionalists one of the key functions of the education system is

B – to cultivate achieved status

Q9 - Althusser (Marxist) argued that the main role of education in a capitalist society was the reproduction of

C – an efficient and obedient work force

Q10 – Bowles and Gintis (Marxists) came up with the concept of 'the correspondence principle'. The correspondence principle recognizes

D - a school's processes as being very similar to those found in offices and factories

Q11 Both functionalist and Marxist perspectives have similarities. They both

A - tend to ignore social processes within school – except Willis

Q12 – Which term does Bourdieu use to describe the cultural characteristics and values of each social class?

B – habitus

Q13 – Cultural capital as identified by Bourdieu refers to:

C – the knowledge, language and values which readily translate into educational capital

Q14 – Cultural differences are extended further by examining sub-cultural differences between social groups. Sugarman and Hyman highlighted the effects of socialization because:

D - the middle classes socialized their children to have future time orientation and deferred gratification

Q15 – Bernstein's research focused on linguistic deprivation and its influence on educational success. Bernstein distinguished between:

C – restricted speech codes and elaborated speech codes

Q16 – Pupil premium is used by the state as a form of:

A – compensatory education

Q17 - Rutter places great emphasis on the way a school organizes itself. The better their organizational structures and polices the better the school. Three of these policies are:

C - marking policy; teacher reward systems; mixed ability classes

Q18 – Bowles and Ginitis talk of the myth of meritocracy. The myth of meritocracy refers to:

C - schools legitimate the myth that everyone has an equal chance

Q19 – The difference between setting and streaming is:

A - setting is where pupils of <u>similar</u> ability are put in different sets (groups) in <u>specific</u> subjects studied, while streaming involves grouping students of <u>similar</u> ability for <u>every</u> subject studied

Q20 – The halo effect is positive stereotype given by teachers to pupils who

C – are enthusiastic and hardworking

Q21 - Rosenthal and Jacobson's (1968) research found positive and negative labels helped produce

B – self-fulfilling prophecy in the classroom

Q22 - Mac an Ghaill (1994) identified 3 working-class male subcultures

D - macho lads; academic achievers; new enterprisers

Q23 – As well as Paul Willis, Colin Lacey's (1970) study of Hightown Grammar school also showed how streaming can lead to the creation of

B – anti-school subculture

Q24 - C. Jackson (2006) 'Lads and Ladettes in School: Gender and the Fear of Failure' looked at how girls are forming anti-school subcultures and becoming

C – ladettes because of the fear of academic failure

Q25 – Complete the sentence: 'Gender is not the strongest predictor of attainment…..'

A – because social class attainment gap at Key Stage 4 is three times as wide as the gender gap and some minority ethnic groups achievement is much greater than the gap between boys and girls.

Q26 - Teacher-pupil interaction affecting the gender gap. Howe (1997) identified the different ways teachers interact with boys and girls - such differences in interaction emerge….

C - very early, even in preschool

Q27 - Masculine identity can be seen as incompatible with academic success. Kelly (1987) found science and the science classroom remain

D - 'masculine' environments with boys dominating science classrooms

Q28 – The term ethnocentric curriculum refers to

A – the school curriculum and the hidden curriculum is too focused on white British culture and adds to the low self-esteem and underachievement of ethnic minorities

Q29 – Family life outside school can affect achievement inside school. Some minority ethnic groups have stronger parental support than others. Chinese students are seen to have high levels of achievement in school because

A – Archer (2006) found Chinese students and parents put a high value on education as it gave the family a high standing in their community

Q30 - Ethnicity and achievement. Highlight which of the following four statements is correct:

D - Stephen J. Ball (2008) found that Black Caribbean and African students are less likely to be identified for gifted and talented programmes. In contrast, evidence also suggests that Chinese and Indian students are more likely to be entered into higher sets

Q31 – Ethnicity and achievement. Highlight which of the following three statements is correct:

B - African-Caribbean and Bangladeshi Asians are more likely to be working-class and in poverty and so have a general material disadvantage while Indian and African Asian children are more likely to come from professional/business middle-class backgrounds and the subsequent advantages

Q32 Ethnicity and attainment. Identify which of the three statements is correct.

A - some ethnic groups, such as Chinese students, have far higher levels of attainment compared to the national level

Q33 – Ethnicity and attainment. Identify which of the three statements is correct.

C - Chinese students are the highest attaining group, with 78.5% achieving 5 A*-C grades including Maths and English. This compares to 70% in 2006/07

Q34 - Ethnicity and attainment. Identify which of the three statements is correct:

C - Bangladeshi pupils now have a slightly higher attainment rate than White pupils, with 59.7% 5 A*-C grades including Maths and English. This is a massive improvement given that only around 40% achieved this 2006/07, which was 5% less than White pupils

Q35 – Ethnicity and attainment. Identify which of the three statements is correct:

B - Travellers, Gypsies and Roma are still the lowest achieving groups, with 17.5% of Irish Travellers and 10.8% of those from Gypsy or Roma backgrounds achieving 5 A*-C grades including Maths and English.

7 **EDUCATION -** SINGLE QUESTIONS

Q1 Identify two reasons why are girls have higher levels of achievement in school than boys

Q2 Identify two reasons why girls have high levels of achievement in school (this question doesn't mention boys)

Q3 Identify two reasons why boys are underachieving in school (this question makes no mention of girls)

Q4 Identify two functions that the education system might perform

Q5 Identify two polices contributing to the marketization of education

Q6 Identify two ways in which cultural deprivation might affect work-class pupil under achievement in school (this question is not asking about material factors)

Q7 Functionalists have their own perspective on the purpose of the education system. Identify two criticisms other sociologists might make of the functionalist perspective.

Q8 Identify three ways in which social policies may have influenced social-class differences in educational achievement

Q9 Identify three factors outside school which may have aided girls' achievement in school (you do not mention factors inside school)

Q10 Identify three factors within schools which may have affect the educational underachievement of some ethnic minority groups.

Q11 – Identify three ways in which Marxists would say the education system and its processes replicate the workplace.

Q12 – Identify three types of school subcultures

Q13 – Identify three reasons why working-class parents might not attend parents' evenings

Q14 - Identify three processes inside school which may have an effect on pupils from different social groups

Q15 - Identify three processes outside school which may have an effect on pupils from different social groups

Q16 – identify one criticism of labelling theory

Q17 – Identify three ways in which a school's curriculum might be ethnocentric

Q18 – Identify two policies designed to encourage the introduction of market forces in the education system

Q19 – Identify two ways in which pupils identities might be shaped by their experiences at school

8 **EDUCATION** - SINGLE QUESTIONS: THE ANSWERS

Q1 Identify two reasons why are girls have higher levels of achievement in school than boys

- the women's movement and feminism raised girls' expectations and self-esteem
- the increasing number of employment opportunities for women
- many girls' mother are in paid employment and act as positive role models for them
- girls' priorities have changed: Sue Sharpe (1976) 'Just Like a Girl'
- girls are better motivated and organised than boys
- girls at 16 are seen to be more mature than boys
- girls benefitted from introduction of coursework in GCSEs/A-Levels
- national curriculum made more subjects compulsory
- teachers less likely to gender stereotype girls into set roles or careers

Q2 Identify two reasons why girls have high levels of achievement in school (this question doesn't mention boys)

- the women's movement and feminism raised girls' expectations and self-esteem
- the increasing number of employment opportunities for women
- many girls' mother are in paid employment and act as positive role models for them
- girls' priorities have changed: Sue Sharpe (1976) 'Just Like a Girl'

Q3 Identify two reasons why boys are underachieving in school (this question makes no mention of girls)

- boys are generally more disruptive in class than girls
- boys appear to gain 'street cred' by not working hard
- decline in traditional male jobs
- teachers tend to have lower expectations of boys
- lack of male role models in schools
- laddish subcultures
- identity crisis in men – uncertain future removes purpose in achieving
- boys do not like reading as it has become feminised
- boys tend to overestimate their ability
- feminisation of assessment – coursework rather than competitive exams

Q4 Identify two functions that the education system might perform

- secondary socialization
- gender role socialization
- division of labour
- role allocation
- establishment of universalistic values
- meritocracy
- value consensus through the hidden curriculum
- meritocracy
- competition

Q5 Identify two polices contributing to the marketization of education

- publication of school league tables showing exam results
- schools competing for pupils
- publication of Ofsted reports
- schools opting out of local authority control
- encouragement of different types of schools - Free Schools; Academies etc
- 1988 Education Reform Act

Q6 Identify two ways in which cultural deprivation might affect work-class pupil under achievement in school (this question is not asking about material factors)

- immediate gratification
- present time orientation
- lack of cultural capital
- parental attitudes to education
- sense of fatalism
- speech and language codes
- parents level of educational achievement

Q7 Functionalists have their own perspective on the purpose of the education system. Identify two criticisms other sociologists might make of the functionalist perspective.

- Marxists point out meritocracy is a myth
- Marxists would point out to functionalists how the role allocation of jobs is not conducted via meritocracy as many jobs are allocated via social-class background
- Marxists would point out to functionalists how the education system does not encourage the sharing of values through consensual processes rather the education system is there to promote a ruling-class ideology
- Paul Willis' would point out how a number of pupils reject the values being taught via the educations system. Instead of passively accepting what is being delivered/communicated they reject it and can form anti-school subcultures

- Feminists would point out the school system encourages gender role allocation eg too few girls choose to study engineering
- Feminists would point out the school system encourages patriarchal gender regimes e.g. many school leadership teams are male dominated

Q8 Identify three ways in which social policies may have influenced social-class differences in educational achievement

- Parental power as consumers of education – sometimes known as parentocracy
- New vocationalism
- Free school meals
- Compensatory education policies
- Correspondence principle
- Expansion of Higher Education
- Marketization
- Private schooling

Q9 Identify three factors outside school which may have aided girls' achievement in school (you do not mention factors inside school)

- Women in paid employment
- Feminism
- Parental encouragement
- Equal opportunities in the workplace – career and pay
- Changing nature of work – more feminized jobs
- Changing patterns of work – more flexible shift work allowing women to balance child-care with paid work
- Increase in divorce rates
- Increase in lone parenting
- Changing girls aspirations
- Different leisure patterns – girls prefer reading/conversation improving their linguistic skills needed for literature based subjects. Much of this comes from be socialized by their mothers reading to them as children

Q10 Identify three factors within schools which may have affect the educational underachievement of some ethnic minority groups.

- self-fulfilling prophecy from teacher labelling
- teacher's negativity
- teacher racism
- ethnocentric curriculum
- discriminatory admission and selection processes
- institutional racism
- anti-school subcultures
- culture of resistance – Hall

Q11 – Identify three ways in which Marxists would say the education system and its processes replicate the workplace.

- Hierarchy of authority
- Correspondence principle
- Both driven by competitive processes
- Class alienation – working class feel alienated in a predominantly middle-class institution
- Status difference – wealthy children go to fee-paying schools (end up having high-flying careers)) while the majority attend state schools (end up having jobs with limited opportunities)
- Reward systems – schools reward good work with 'stars' & 'merits' which is replicated in work-place to relieve the monotony
- Fragmented timetable learning – work – break-time – back to work – break-time – back to work

Q12 – Identify three types of school subcultures

- Male anti-school subcultures
- Female school subcultures
- African-Caribbean male subcultures
- African-Caribbean female subcultures

Q13 – Identify three reasons why working-class parents might not attend parents' evenings

- Lack of interest
- Feeling of inferiority against predominantly middle-class teachers
- More likely to be on shift-work than middle-class parents
- Having to work longer hours to compensate for low pay
- Can't afford child-minder in order to attend
- Lack of education themselves so unable to understand subject based targets set by the teacher

Q14 - Identify three processes inside school which may have an effect on pupils from different social groups

- Labelling
- Halo effect
- Self-fulfilling prophecy
- Ethnocentric curriculum
- Setting/streaming
- Mixed ability classes
- Subcultures
- School organization
- Gender regimes
- Open enrolment

Q15 - Identify three processes outside school which may have an effect on pupils from different social groups

- Material deprivation
- Cultural deprivation
- Speech codes

- Parental interest
- Parental education
- Parental occupation
- Cultural capital – habitus
- Compensatory education
- Marketization – choosing school via income – postcode lottery

Q16 – identify one criticism of labelling theory

- Too deterministic – some pupils remove the labels through hard work
- Ignores other influences – e.g. material deprivation
- Doesn't consider the influence of wider society in the construction of labels given out in classroom e.g. race
- Assumes pupils are aware they have been labelled – some aren't
- Assumes there's always a self-fulfilling prophecy – some pupils ignore the label

Q17 – Identify three ways in which a school's curriculum might be ethnocentric

- Not providing Halal meals
- History lesson too focused on White history
- School holidays constructed around Christian calendar
- Religious assemblies delivered from a singular religious perspective
- Uniform and dress codes designed around Western values
- Dress/changing rooms for PE and Games lessons structured around Western values

Q18 – Identify two policies designed to encourage the introduction of market forces in the education system

- The National Curriculum
- National testing (SATS)
- National league tables
- Open enrolment and parental choice
- Ofsted
- Local management of schools
- Schools having control of their own admissions criteria
- Schools having their own discipline and exclusion criteria

Q19 – Identify two ways in which pupils identities might be shaped by their experiences at school

- Subject choice – though national curriculum aimed to limit differences between gender regimes in subject choice physics, chemistry and Maths are still seen as male subjects while art, English and dance are seen as girl subjects
- Gender socialization – gender stereotypes were still found in many school books
- Gender socialization - masculine identity can be seen as incompatible with academic success
- Pupil subcultures
- Teacher-pupil interaction affecting the gender gap
- Differing rates of achievement – girls outperforming boys due to wider social changes
- feminization of assessment – coursework rather than competitive exams
- gendered language
- women in the curriculum

9 RESEARCH METHODS - MULTIPLE CHOICE QUESTIONS

Q1 - Positivists prefer to collect quantitative data through the following research methods which are seen to collect reliable data

A - Informal interviews; open-ended questionnaires; data from diaries

B - Data from diaries and letters; informal interviews; open-ended questionnaires;

C- Laboratory experiments; social surveys; structured questionnaires; use of official statistics

D - Participant and non-participant observations

Q2 - Interpretivists use the term verstehen to describe their data gathering processes. Verstehen means:

A – achieving an empathetic understanding of people by seeing the world from their perspective

B – achieving an empathetic understanding of people by recording their gender, age, sexuality and ethnicity

C – achieving an empathetic understanding of people by giving them a structured questionnaire to complete

D – asking people to complete a postal questionnaire within a designated period of time

Q3 – The difference between primary and secondary sources of data is…

A – Primary data collected by sociologists themselves while secondary data is data which already exists such as that found in newspapers, novels etc.

B – Secondary data collected by sociologists themselves while primary data is data which already exists such as that found in newspapers, novels etc.

C – Primary data is collect first and secondary data is collected second.

D – Primary data is quantitative sources and secondary data is qualitative sources

Q4 - When doing research sociologists always consider the ethics of what they are doing because

A – sociologists are 'right-on' sort of people

B – sociologists are concerned with morality (what is right and wrong) when undertaking research

C – sociologists are seeking the truth through research methods

D – sociologists are concerned about getting to the truth through any means possible

Q5 – When sociologists talk about validity they are concerned with:

A – their chosen method is repeatable

B – their chosen method is ethical

C – their chosen method being representative

D – their chosen method uncovering the truth

Q6 – When sociologists talk about a sampling-frame they are referring to:

A - the whole group being studied

B – a type of sample method select from which to draw their data

C – where they will gather their data in order to make certain it is a representative sample

D - a list of names of all those included in the survey population from which the sample is selected

Q7 – A representative sample is

A – is chosen from a subdivided group of people e.g. a specific age range in order to cover a reasonable cross-section of the group being surveyed

B – selects people at random in order to cover a reasonable cross-section of the group being surveyed

C - is a smaller group taken from the population being surveyed in to cover a reasonable cross-section of the group being surveyed

D – is about selecting from the sampling frame at regular intervals until the size of sample is reached

Q8 – When sociologists conduct social surveys they usually use

A – open interviews and observations

B – a unique sampling method

C – questionnaires or structured interviews

D – a unique research method

Q9 – When sociologists conduct field experiments they

A – carry them out in the real world conditions, such as a school, while at the same time trying to follow similar procedures to those found in any laboratory experiment

B – carry them out on school playing fields or similar surroundings, while at the same time trying to follow similar procedures to those found in any laboratory experiment

C – carry them out in the real world conditions, such as a school, while at the same time trying not to follow similar procedures to those found in any laboratory experiment

D - carry them out on school playing fields or similar surroundings, while at the same time trying not to follow similar procedures to those found in any laboratory experiment

Q10 – One problem of using the experimental method in sociology is

A – the Hawthorne Effect

B- the sample method

C – the comparative method

D – the viral effect

Q11 – Which type of sociologists prefer to use the social survey method?

A – interpretivists

B – field experimentalists

C – positivists

D – qualitativists

Q12 – Social surveys cause three distinct problems for sociologists

A – validity, generalisation, reliability

B – validity, replicability, desirability

C – validity, ethics, replicability

D – validity, victimology, methodology

Q13 When sociologists' talk of the imposition problem, they are referring to:

A – the limited availability of respondents imposing artificial limits on the data available for collection

B – the limited availability of prepared questions imposing artificial limits on the data available for collection

C – the limited choice of answers imposing artificial limits on the data available for collection

D – the limited amount of time available to the respondent imposing artificial limits on the data available for collection

Q14 – Pre-coded questionnaires are those with

A – have no structure

B – leave the respondent free to complete in a manner they feel appropriate

C – are highly structured

D – leave enough room for the respondent to write the minimum of two sentences

Q15 – Postal questionnaires are

A – tend to be sent through the post to the respondent

B – tend to left at the Post-Office for the respondent to collect

C – tend to be sent through the post to the respondent along with a pre-paid addressed envelope

D – are no longer used by sociologists due to the rising cost of postage

Q16 One problem with postal questionnaires is

A – not enough respondents collect them from the Post-Office to make the survey results valid and representative

B – you can't ask any embarrassing questions

C – because there's a return-envelope the sociologists gets more data than they can process

D – there is never any way of knowing who completed the questionnaire causing major problems for the validity and representativeness of the results

Q17 – One problem with the validity of research conducted through the use of open - questionnaires is:

A – they are quick to repeat

B – participant observations are more valid

C – they produce reliable data

D – the range of answers can be so broad they're difficult to quantify

Q18 – Content analysis involves:

A – involves the analysis of 'messages' in mass media content such as TV programmes, newspapers, magazines etc (secondary sources) which can generate both quantitative and qualitative data

B - involves the analysis of 'messages' of just TV (secondary sources) content which can generate both quantitative and qualitative data

C - involves the analysis of 'messages' of just newspaper content (secondary sources) which can generate both quantitative and qualitative data

D - involves the analysis of 'messages' in mass media content such as TV programmes, newspapers, magazines etc (secondary sources) which can generate only qualitative data

Q 19 One weakness of conducting content analysis is

A - Low cost

B - Time consuming

C - Can make comparisons over time (longitudinal study)

D - Quantitative analysis is seen as reliable

Q 20 - Triangulation sometimes referred to as methodological pluralism is

A – the formation of a triangular structure from quantitative data in order to assess the validity of a method

B – the formation of triangular structure from qualitative data in order to assess the validity of a method

C - is the use of one or more research method when carrying out social research in order for the different methods to complement each other

D - is the use of one or more research method when carrying out social research in order for the different methods to challenge each other

Q21 – Overt observations is where

A - the researcher will disclose themselves to the participants so they know they're being observed

B – the researcher hides themselves from the participants so they don't know they're being observed

C – the researcher participates in what they're observing

D – the researcher doesn't participate in what they're observing

Q22 – When a researcher says their method is reliable they mean

A – their chosen method is concerned with seeking the truth

B – their chosen method is concerned about what is right or wrong in the research process

C – their chosen method means if another researcher conducted the same method with the same respondents they would achieve the same results

D – their chosen method is collecting primary data because it is more valid

Q23 – Longitudinal studies are studies which are:

A – conducted at regular interval with a small sample

B – conducted at regular intervals over a short period of time

C – conducted at regular intervals over a long period of time

D – conducted at regular intervals over a moderate period of time

Q24 Secondary qualitative data, is data which

A – already exists such as official statistics like crime rates

B – has to be gathered by the researchers such as through interviews

C – has to be gathered on a longitudinal basis such as school league tables

D – already exists such as diary entries

Q25 – Positivists question the reliability of participant observation because

A – they are easy to replicate and subsequently check the validity of any findings

B – they are difficult to replicate and so check the validity of any findings

C – they are difficult to replicate and subsequently improves the validity of any findings

D – they are not interested in replication

Q26 – Ethnographic studies are

A – are seen as valid as the research is conducted in a laboratory setting

B – are seen as valid as the research is conducted using closed questionnaires

C- are seen as valid as the research is conducted in a natural setting

D – are seen as valid as the research is conducted using structured interviews

Q27 – Case studies usually involve the use of

A – the experimental method particularly field experiments

B – positivist methods such as structured interviews or closed questionnaires

C - interpretivist methods such as open-interviews or participant observations

D – content analysis involving the analysis of media messages

Q28 – Triangulation can be referred to as

A – methodological ambiguity

B – methodological determinism

C – methodological singularity

D – methodological pluralism

Q29 – Longitudinal studies are studies which

A – collect data regularly once a week

B – collect data at regular intervals over a period of years

C – collect data at regular periods over a month

D – collect data at regular periods over a year

Q30 – There are three types of experiments sociologists can use

A – the laboratory, field and clandestine experiment

B – the laboratory, field and open experiment

C – the laboratory, field and natural experiment

D - the laboratory, field and closed experiment

Q31 – Field experiments are those which

A – occur in school playing fields while trying to follow similar procedures to those found in any laboratory experiment

B- occur in real-life conditions such as a school while trying to follow similar procedures to those found in any laboratory experiment

C - occur in real-life conditions such as a school while trying to follow similar procedures to those found in all sociological research

D - occur in real-life conditions such as a school while trying to follow similar procedures to those found in all social science research

Q32 – One criticism of official statistics is they are sometimes

A – massaged by the sociologist in order to avoid embarrassment if they have done something wrong

B – they are too complex to put into readable graphs or charts

C – massaged by the state to avoid embarrassing the government of the day

D – they are not in-depth enough to be put into readable graphs or charts

10 **RESEARCH METHODS** - MULTIPLE CHOICE ANSWERS

Q1 - Positivists prefer to collect quantitative data through the following research methods which are seen to collect reliable data

C- Laboratory experiments; social surveys; structured questionnaires; use of official statistics

Q2 - Interpretivists use the term verstehen to describe their data gathering processes. Verstehen means:

A – achieving an empathetic understanding of people by seeing the world from their perspective

Q3 – The difference between primary and secondary sources of data is...

A – Primary data collected by sociologists themselves while secondary data is data which already exists such as that found in newspapers, novels etc.

Q4 - When doing research sociologists always consider the ethics of what they are doing because

B – sociologists are concerned with morality (what is right and wrong) when undertaking research

Q5 – When sociologists talk about validity they are concerned with:

D – their chosen method uncovering the truth

Q6 – When sociologists talk about a sampling-frame they are referring to:

D - a list of names of all those included in the survey population from which the sample is selected

Q7 – A representative sample is

C - is a smaller group taken from the population being surveyed in to cover a reasonable cross-section of the group being surveyed

Q8 – When sociologists conduct social surveys they usually use

C – questionnaires or structured interviews

Q9 – When sociologists conduct field experiments they

A – carry them out in the real world conditions, such as a school, while at the same time trying to follow similar procedures to those found in any laboratory experiment

Q10 – One problem of using the experimental method in sociology is

A – the Hawthorne Effect

Q11 – Which type of sociologists prefer to use the social survey method?

C – positivists

Q12 – Social surveys cause three distinct problems for sociologists

A – validity, generalization, reliability

Q13 When sociologists' talk of the imposition problem, they are referring to:

C – the limited choice of answers imposing artificial limits on the data available for collection

Q14 – Pre-coded questionnaires are those with

C – are highly structured

Q15 – Postal questionnaires are

C – tend to be sent through the post to the respondent along with a pre-paid addressed envelope

Q16 One problem with postal questionnaires is

D – there is never any way of knowing who completed the questionnaire causing major problems for the validity and representativeness of the results

Q17 – One problem with the validity of research conducted through the use of open - questionnaires is:

D – the range of answers can be so broad they're difficult to quantify

Q18 – Content analysis involves:

A – involves the analysis of 'messages' in mass media content such as TV programmes, newspapers, magazines etc (secondary sources) which can generate both quantitative and qualitative data

Q 19 One weakness of conducting content analysis is

B - Time consuming

Q 20 - Triangulation sometimes referred to as methodological pluralism is

C - is the use of one or more research method when carrying out social research in order for the different methods to complement each other

Q21 – Overt observations is where

A - the researcher will disclose themselves to the participants so they know they're being observed

Q22 – When a researcher says their method is reliable they mean

C – their chosen method means if another researcher conducted the same method with the same respondents they would achieve the same results

Q23 – Longitudinal studies are studies which are:

C – conducted at regular intervals over a long period of time

Q24 Secondary qualitative data, is data which

D – already exists such as diary entries

Q25 – Positivists question the reliability of participant observation because

B – they are difficult to replicate and so check the validity of any findings

Q26 – Ethnographic studies are

C- are seen as valid as the research is conducted in a natural setting

Q27 – Case studies usually involve the use of

C - interpretivist methods such as open-interviews or participant observations

Q28 – Triangulation is usually referred to as

D – methodological pluralism

Q29 – Longitudinal studies are studies which

B – collect data at regular intervals over a period of years

Q30 – There are three types of experiments sociologists can use

C – the laboratory, field and natural experiment

Q31 – Field experiments occur

B- in real-life conditions such as a school while trying to follow similar procedures to those found in any laboratory experiment

Q32 – One criticism of official statistics is they are sometimes

C – massaged by the state to avoid embarrassing the government of the day

ABOUT THE AUTHOR

The contents of the book have been written by sociologytwynham.com. For any other information or question you would like answering please contact us via the website. For other information on books in the series please visit the Revision page at sociologytwynham.com.